HOW TO POO
ON A DATE

Published in 2014 by Prion Books
An imprint of the Carlton Publishing Group
20 Mortimer Street
London W1T 3JW

A CIP catalogue record for this book is available from the British Library

ISBN 978-1-85375-782-2

Printed in China

HOW TO POO ON A DATE

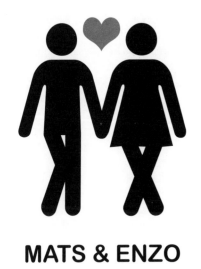

MATS & ENZO

PRION

We will begin this book with the story of Tom G. His was a typical story: adrenaline-fuelled first date, then several months of full seduction arsenal deployment in order to gain the affections of Amy. It worked: he managed to completely conquer her. He felt perfectly secure in his new relationship. For him, this was it: Amy was his forever. For Tom this also meant he could finally stop trying to keep the mystery alive. Why not? She was his and he knew it. He was so confident in the strength of his relationship with Amy that it seemed perfectly normal to him to now hold a conversation with her with the toilet door open while relieving himself unperturbed, shouting things like: "Wait for me, honey, it's a go for take-off, five minutes and we're ready to launch!"

Tom G. committed a monumental error of judgement, one that he is still paying for: Tom G. is now single.

SUPERHUMAN

One of the secrets of seduction (and this goes as much for a first date as for the rest of the relationship) is to stay faultless at all times. However, you are made of flesh and bone and this means that yes, sometimes you have to go to the loo. This vital human requirement remains strangely taboo in modern society, and it can ruin a blooming or well-established relationship in an instant. It also illustrates superbly the inherent ambiguity of love: you are a god (or goddess) in your darling's eyes, and yet also a mere mortal, who once or twice a day is overcome by an uncontrollable urge to go to the toilet as quickly as possible. And if s/he idealises you, that inevitably means that s/he has never seen you walking funny because you are clenching your buttocks with all your might, with only one thought in your head: "Please let me make it! Please let me make it!"

The only way to ensure the harmonious survival of long-term relationships, or to make sure that a first date won't be also be the last, is to portray at all times the image of a superhuman who never (or almost never) goes to the toilet. But you guessed it: it's not easy.

However, fear not: this is where we come in.

We have firmly established that all the commonly-used techniques to hide the true nature of our sudden absences due to toilet-related urges don't work anymore. There is the old "I'm going to powder my nose" which may have worked a century ago, but don't even try it nowadays. Another popular phrase that everyone can see right through is "Excuse me, I must go wash my hands." Saying "I just need to step out for a minute" is about as subtle as shouting "Excuse me while I take a dump."

In the absence of these good old excuses, what else can you do? As the great statesman – and, so our sources say, an expert toilet user – Winston Churchill would have said: it's a riddle wrapped in a mystery inside an enigma.

Not any more, Winston, not anymore.

We have devoted five years of our lives to researching this predicament and have come up with many new techniques that will help you smoothly out of any such potentially maladroit – and malodorous – situations. This book demonstrates them all.

YOU ARE MOST WELCOME

Secondly, let us elaborate on how (and why) you should use this book. The reason that we threw ourselves into this monumental project was simple: we could no longer allow something as banal as going to the toilet to continue to destroy millions of perfectly good relationships anally all over the world. We are aware that the oblivious among you will find the subject of this book whimsical. These insouciant souls should know that a Japanese study recently made this shocking discovery: the reason for a substantial drop in the birth rate on this particular archipelago is largely due to unhelpful toilet use by the Japanese. This is easier to understand once you know that typical Japanese dwellings have paper-thin walls, forcing the spouse or partner to hear (and sometimes feel) each and every sound of the ongoing operation!

IT'S ALL ABOUT THE TOILET

Before we begin to unveil all of our powerful and dazzling techniques, we ask that you pause and think for a minute about your own past heartbreaking failures. There was surely a reason behind those breakups? Stop fooling yourself by thinking that s/he "just wasn't the one for you". Stop looking for reasons outside of yourself and begin by asking yourself the right questions: Did I always do the right thing when I used the toilet in my sweetheart's presence? Why did my last girlfriend/boyfriend's attitude suddenly change just as I was experiencing a violent bout of gastroenteritis?

In our research we have found that in 97.8% of all breakups the reason for the death of the relationship hides in the answers to these questions. If only you had discovered this book before it was too late! You would probably never have known what failure in love feels like.

YOU WILL NO LONGER STINK AT LOVE!

However, don't dwell on past mistakes. By deciding to read this book you have made an important and life-changing decision: with its help, you will forever change your romantic relations, and with that, your entire life! This book will help you succeed in love. You will understand the pitfalls you must avoid, and make those precious first steps towards a new beginning. Anything will be possible if you just make that effort.

We won't lie – the road ahead is long and sometimes difficult. But you have in us two trustworthy and knowledgeable friends who will guide you through all the toilet conundrums you'll encounter in your life and love. Your toilet trips will soon no longer be an obstacle to the happiness you deserve.

In order to keep this promise we have chosen an original approach to give you solutions to every toilet dilemma, be it in an established relationship or during those difficult first dates. We will tackle all situations, even the really tricky ones such as romantic walks or posh restaurants, as well as demonstrating effective techniques to employ to stop you from taking too long.

A NOTE ON GENDER USE IN THIS BOOK

Women are much more advanced in their toilet behaviour than men, having successfully perpetuated the myth that they never poo or fart. That said, we are convinced that some of the advice in this book will also serve them on more than one occasion as well. All the situations that we have tackled could also be encountered by the fairer sex. However, we are gentlemen, and we certainly don't want to mess with the female 'we-no-poo' narrative, that we have always applauded and admire. That is why we wrote this book from a man's perspective. Could a testimony from a Paul actually be from a Paula? A gentleman never tells.

Man or woman, if you have to take one thing from this introduction, it would be: have faith in us. We promise we will make your romantic relationships longer, and stronger, by giving you all the tools you need to ensure problem-free toilet visits forever!

MATS & ENZO

THE NINE GOLDEN RULES

There are nine rules that should never be broken in the course of any relationship. Disobeying even just one of these rules could put your relationship or date – and their long-term potential – at peril.

1. **SECRECY**: Never say precisely what you are going to do.

    Example – Do not say: "Darling, I have to go and recycle that delicious lunch you cooked".

2. **INTIMACY**: Always go alone.

    Example – Never say: "Will you come to the toilet with me, honey?"

3. **INVISIBILITY**: Make sure nobody sees you enter or come out.

    Example – Don't get caught running down the corridor with your trousers around your ankles, no matter how badly you need to go.

4. **SILENCE**: Don't give any indication upon your return as to what's just occurred.

    Example – Do not say: "Ah, I feel two pounds (0.9kg) lighter!"

5. **IDENTITY**: Come back in the exact same configuration you left in (same clothes, same hair, clean hands…)

    Example – Don't come back with your shirt stuck in your zip, and most definitely never ask for her help with it.

6. SECURITY: Don't reveal any clues that could give away the purpose of your mission.

>**Example** – Don't walk to the bathroom with a gossip magazine and packet of Anusol in your hands.

7. SPEED: Never be away for more than five minutes, to avoid all suspicion.

>**Example** – Do not stay in the toilet for an hour, no matter how much you are enjoying it, or how necessary it may be.

8. COMPOSURE: Never show how you feel.

>**Example** – Do not walk to the toilet with your buttocks clenched and your hands pressed to your bum whilst moaning out loud.

9. MODESTY: Never brag.

>**Example** – Do not say: "Darling, you would be proud of me, I just pushed out a real rim-splitter!"

A WORD FROM THE EXPERT

I am a psychologist specializing in toilet-related trauma and dysfunction, so I was thrilled to see that Mats and Enzo were finally publishing the first comprehensive guide on how to use the toilet when one is in love or on a date. Ever since *How To Poo At Work* came out I was convinced that the same book should be written about such issues in romantic relationships. I have stopped counting the number of people who have turned to me for help after they were dumped because they did not respect one of the nine golden rules of toilet behaviour. I wholeheartedly thank the authors for unveiling the secrets of how to properly go to the toilet when in a relationship.

On the following pages, you will be able to read my precious advice. I participated in the creation of this book as an expert and consultant, and I will accompany you in your discovery and mastery of these new techniques. You may already be familiar with my husband Tom Hayatt, the world expert on toilet behaviour while at work. (He was involved as the expert adviser in Mats and Enzo's first book *How To Poo At Work*.) My husband is known around the world as the best man to do his deed at work. I, on the other hand, am the master of techniques required to go to the toilet without leaving a trace. I met my husband at a joint workshop where we, as the world's most eminent toilet experts, were invited to give a speech on the sidelines of a G8 summit for all the leaders of the free world, entitled: "Conflict resolution through diplomatic toilet use." The heads of state were enthralled by all the techniques we taught them, while sparks flew between Tom and I. This was over 20 years ago, and our relationship is stronger than ever, thanks mainly to our mastery of problem-free toilet use!

But back to the subject at hand. I have never found any scientific study nor popular psychology book that would approach the problem of toilet use in a couple as pertinently as Mats and Enzo do in their new book. While books such as *Men Are From Mars, Women Are From Venus* reveal some interesting truths, they are completely useless if you do not master going to the loo when you are in a romantic relationship.

I urge you therefore to read this book. By failing to do so, you expose yourself to great risks in your relationships or dates. I am convinced that it will save you many future heartaches. I truly believe in Mats and Enzo's claim that bad toilet training can ruin even the most solid of relationships. I cannot insist strongly enough that it is absolutely vital that you learn and memorize all the techniques in this book. You'll be thankful you did. And so will your spouse or partner.

KAREN HAYATT

CONTENTS

Part 1: Romantic Dates and Walks

PART 1: ROMANTIC WALKS / DATES

How do you do your deed safely when taking a romantic walk?

Say you are enjoying a gondola ride in Venice. You can't very well say to the gondolier: "Scusami, voglio andare alla toilette, se possibile…"

Similarly, when you are riding horses together in the country, you will surely get incredibly frustrated with the horses who do their business, right in front of you, whenever and wherever, while you are doing your best to hold it in.

Don't worry. We've made a list of all the tricky situations that you will experience during an important date or romantic encounter when the sudden urge to have a poo takes hold. Here are all the solutions you'll need…

ON A TANDEM

You are enjoying a countryside getaway. After renting a tandem bicycle you decide to ride to the nearby farm to buy fresh eggs. You are enjoying the fresh air, the wind caressing your body… But the pedalling is stimulating your abdominals, and you know this means that you must go to the toilet immediately.

DIFFICULTY

★ ★ ★ ★ ★

SOLUTION: TAKING A BACK SEAT

1. Don't say anything to your partner about the mission you must accomplish (SECRECY rule).
2. Take a seat at the back of the bicycle and insist that she respect the three rules of the captain (tandem front-seat rider): "1: Never take your eyes off the road. 2: Never take your eyes off the road. 3: Never take your eyes off the road."
3. Silently and discreetly unbutton your trousers.
4. Lift yourself up slightly and pull down your trousers as well as your underpants.
5. Sit on top of the basket at the back of the bicycle and quickly do your deed (SPEED rule). (Important: hold on to the seat so as to not lose your balance.)
6. Once you finish, put your trousers back on and ride on normally.
7. Throw the basket to the side of the road while continuing to pedal.

EXPERT'S OPINION

"One of my patients used this technique. When he sat on the basket, his belt got stuck in the chain and he very nearly lost his manhood. I think you can understand why he needed my help afterwards..."

TESTIMONIAL

"To cover up the give-away noises I started to sing a rude song. She laughed so hard it brought tears to her eyes and she lost control of the tandem. After a very messy crash in the gutter she decided not to see me again."

Julian, 32, single (recently), Bristol

PARKLOVE

You are taking a walk in the park. You are enjoying the smell of pine and lavender, but they remind you of your toilet air freshener 'Provence lavender forest breeze'. The outdoor activity, paired with familiar smells, triggers something and, all of a sudden, you need to go to the toilet – fast.

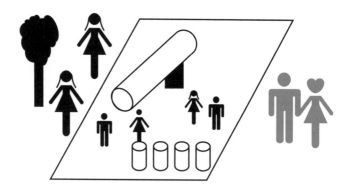

DIFFICULTY

SOLUTION: DOWNHILL RUN

1. Go to a children's playground, telling your partner that it is important to stay young at heart.
2. Go towards the tubular slide. Enter.
3. Once inside, stabilise yourself: block your arms and legs against the borders of the slide in order not to slide down.
4. Now that you are hidden from view, you can do your deed.
5. For technical reasons which we need not elaborate on here, come back out by the top of the slide.
6. As you are coming out, complain loudly: "Aaargh! Disgusting! One of the little buggers let one go in the slide! There are two enormous turds in there!"
7. Pick a random child in the playground. Accuse them of being the perpetrator. Drag them over to their mother and tell her exactly what you think of her and how badly she has raised her child. Your partner will see the potential authoritative and responsible future parent in you.

EXPERT'S OPINION

"In such a situation, never go on the swings, not even for a few seconds. I have found in my trials that swings are very good at flinging poo at great speeds in a multitude of directions. It will make the situation worse!"

TESTIMONIAL

"I am a bit chubby and I got stuck inside the slide. It took firemen specialized in emergency earthquake rescue six hours to get me out."

Giles, 29, single, Grimsby

IN AN AIRPLANE, DURING YOUR FIRST ROMANTIC WEEKEND AWAY

You organized a romantic weekend abroad for the two of you. The plane has just taken off. Right after the meal is served, you feel cramps in your stomach. Unfortunately there are two more hours of flight, and you cannot wait till you are at the airport. You will have to go in the tiny airplane toilet.

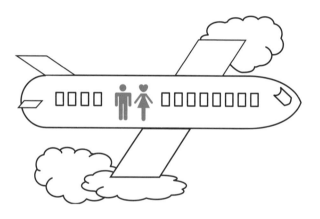

DIFFICULTY

SOLUTION: THE KNEE-JERK

1. Come closer to her.
2. Ask her if she knows what the 'knee-jerk reflex' is.
3. She won't. Slide one hand under her thigh and squeeze very strongly at her knee.
4. The pain will make her scream and she will jump up in her seat.
5. Jump up with her and try to spill as much of your meal as you can.
6. Say: "Wow, I can't believe that you reacted this strongly, you should see someone about it!"
7. Tell her that you need to go clean up your clothes.
8. Since the only water is in the toilet, go and have a poo at more than 800 km/h (Aero SPEED rule).
9. Flush without fear, you will not be vacuumed in.

EXPERT'S OPINION

"Personally I never go to the toilet in an airplane. It's used too frequently. Ugh, warm toilet seats... no, thank you!"

TESTIMONIAL

"I fly at least once a week for work. I will share my little trick with you. When my neighbour farts, I press on all the buttons on the ceiling at the same time. It makes the oxygen mask drop. I use it to breathe while the odour dissipates."

Anthony, 33, in a relationship, Liverpool

IN A GONDOLA

You are desperately trying to be romantic so you agree to the obligatory gondola ride in Venice. Your paramour is discovering the richness of the renaissance architecture. You, on the other hand, would just like to discover a toilet.

DIFFICULTY

SOLUTION: THE BEAUTY IS ELSEWHERE

1. Board the gondola and sit facing her.
2. Look at her tenderly.
3. Pretend you are a bit cold and ask for a blanket. Put it on your knees.
4. Take advantage of being seated, and covered by the blanket, to do your deed on the gondola floor.
5. Once you finish, discreetly put your trousers back on.
6. From then on, do everything you can to shorten the ride.

EXPERT'S OPINION

."If you have a tendency to grimace while you are taking a poo, put on the Venetian mask that you'd bought in the souvenir shop."

TESTIMONIAL

"We were just leaving the gondola when the gondolier took his blanket back. We learned all sorts of swear words in Italian."

James, 52, single, Stoke-on-Trent

HORSEBACK RIDE

You are on a horseback ride in a forest. After a few minutes, the regular quivering in the saddle unleashes a very urgent need to go to the toilet. You just can't wait.

DIFFICULTY

★ ★ ★ ★ ★

SOLUTION: THE RODEO

1. Approach her horse.
2. Whip it violently in its genital area. The pain will make the horse gallop away for at least three minutes, which gives you time to do your mission that can only be done when you are alone (INTIMACY rule).
3. Stop and get down from the horse.
4. Do your deed quickly on the forest floor (SPEED rule) and cover the evidence with twigs and leaves. Jump back on the horse.
5. Gallop towards her.
6. Continue the ride as if nothing out of the ordinary has happened (SILENCE rule).

EXPERT'S OPINION

"Gentlemen, a piece of advice: never brag that you are 'hung like a horse' when an actual horse is present. There's little chance she won't find it amusing."

TESTIMONIAL

"I used this technique... I smacked the horse with my whip, but since it was a mare it didn't work. Instead, it made my girlfriend think that I am some kind of S&M weirdo with zoophile tendencies. She won't talk to me anymore and won't reply to any of my texts..."

Marc, single, 30, Shrewsbury

A BOAT RIDE

You are rowing a boat with your sweetheart on board. You are gliding gently on the water, but the abdominal cramping just won't go away. You are too far from the water's edge for a swift return, and you need to find a solution promptly.

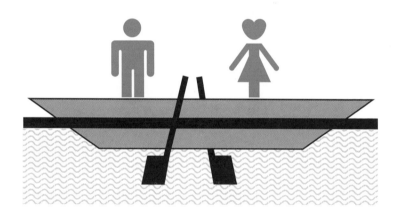

SOLUTION: THE OUTBOARD MOTOR

1. Tell them to sit in front of the boat and put their feet in the water.
2. Go all the way to the back of the boat and sit just above the area where the rudder is, with your bum hovering above the water.
3. The sideboard will serve as a seat and your partner as counterweight. The boat will be sufficiently balanced to allow you to do your business.
4. Do your deed without falling in the water.
5. Cover up any sounds of the poo dropping into the water by coughing loudly at the right time.
6. If the position permits and if your arms are long enough, rinse your bum with some water; you will feel cleaner and nicely refreshed.

EXPERT'S OPINION

"Be careful not to make motor sounds while you're at it."

TESTIMONIAL

"She turned around while I was doing it... She was so shocked that she pushed me in the water with her paddle."

Leo, 28, single, London

ON THE BEACH

You are taking a romantic walk on the beach. The sunset is magnificent. A warm breeze is caressing you and the setting is idyllic. She loves it and doesn't want this evening to end. You, however, want it over already, since it has been more than an hour that you've had the chronic urge to go to the toilet.

DIFFICULTY

★ ★ ★ ★ ★

SOLUTION: IN THE MOONLIGHT

1. Suggest skinny dipping – right there, right then.
2. Once in the water, swim some distance from her and quickly relieve yourself.
3. Leave the area (reminder: it floats).
4. Even if you're tempted, don't stop to examine your poo.

EXPERT'S OPINION

"You can wipe with seaweed, but choose carefully. Certain seaweed found in tropical waters can provoke a horrible rash, while some others can give you spectacular inflammations."

TESTIMONIAL

"I used a type of seaweed in the Bahamas to wipe with, afterwards. My bum quadrupled in size. Other hotel guests nicknamed me hippo."

Marc, 29, in a relationship, Leeds

ON A HORSE-DRAWN CARRIAGE

You are travelling somewhere in Europe and you decide to surprise her with a ride around an old town in a horse-drawn carriage. She loves it, and enjoys being transported a few centuries back in time, in the middle of the verdant surroundings, comfortably seated in the carriage drawn by two beautiful horses. You, on the other hand, only want to be transported in a hurry to a toilet.

DIFFICULTY

SOLUTION: THE GASSY HORSE

1. There is no way you could relieve yourself in this situation. We will therefore explain how, by breaking wind, you can temporarily get some respite until the ride is over.
2. Observe the horse carefully to catch the signals that he is about to pass gas: ears pointing upwards, buttocks relaxing, tail hair that starts to tremble.
3. Once you master these biological characteristics, pass your own gas in the same manner as the horse. This will liberate some space in your conduit and make you feel better and more confident.
4. Repeat the operation until the end of the ride.
5. Blame the horse for any, and all, smells.

EXPERT'S OPINION

"A tip for the most desperate: don't even think of taking the place of the cabman in order to do it in the leather satchel that collects the horses' excrement!"

TESTIMONIAL

"I remember that our cabman couldn't stand the odour of dozens of pounds of horse poo that he had under his nose all day. He tweaked a fire extinguisher to make a giant toilet air freshener for the horses. Every five minutes he sprayed several litres of the lemon-mint freshener into the air."

Paul, 28, in a relationship, Dundee

BONFIRE ON THE BEACH

You are enjoying a romantic evening on the beach, and have built a fire to grill freshly caught lobster. At the end of the meal, the lobsters start to punish your stomach. She is enjoying the romantic moment cuddling up next to you, while your only wish is to find the nearest toilet.

DIFFICULTY

SOLUTION: THE FIRE OF LOVE

1. Stir the fire a bit and pretend you burnt your hand.
2. Run to the sea and throw yourself into the waves.
3. When you're in the water, take off your trousers and do your deed.
4. Return to the beach (while observing the IDENTITY rule) and dry your clothes by the fire.

EXPERT'S OPINION

"Naturally, this technique is to be avoided in a transparent blue lagoon, especially when suffering from a travel bug!"

TESTIMONIAL

"When I came back to the beach, she suggested a midnight dip. Knowing what I had just done in there, I suggested it'd be best to call it a night..."

Lucas, 28, married, eight children, Devonshire

PEDALO ON A LAKE

You are on a pedalo, in the middle of an enormous lake. She loves being close to you but far away from everything else. You? Not right at that moment.

DIFFICULTY

★ ★ ★ ★ ★

SOLUTION: EXTREME SPORTS

1. Tell her you are too hot.
2. Take off your clothes and jump in the water.
3. Discreetly lower your pants in the water.
4. Do your deed. Don't forget to position yourself in a way that the said deed will float under the pedalo (reminder: it floats up immediately).
5. Pull your pants back on.
6. Climb back on the pedalo.
7. Leave the polluted zone as fast as you can, and make sure that your pedalo's blades don't project your poo into the air and onto another boat that might be behind you.

EXPERT'S OPINION

"You should keep in mind that the most difficult thing in this technique is to keep your head above water while you are at it."

TESTIMONIAL

"She decided to join me in the water at the worst possible moment…"
Kieran, 29, single, Easingwold

PEDAL CAR

You rent a pedal car to go for a ride on the embankment by the sea. The repetitive effort to make the car move has stimulated your intestinal transit. This makes you pedal faster and faster, hoping that you will find a toilet quicker, but despite your desperate efforts none are anywhere to be seen...

DIFFICULTY

★ ★ ★ ★ ★

SOLUTION: THE PARIS/DAKAR

1. Keep going fast; you will need the speed...
2. Turn towards the beach and ride on the sand.
3. Even though this is becoming increasingly difficult, you should keep up your speed in order not to sink into the sand and get stuck.
4. Pretend you have to avoid a child and make a sharp turn, launching both of you into the water.
5. Once both of you and the car are in the water, check if she is alright and tell her that you will get the car out of the water by yourself.
6. Kneeling in the water, pretend you are taking off a wheel and take advantage of this time to do your deed.

EXPERT'S OPINION

"Think ahead: rent an off-road pedal car!"

TESTIMONIAL

"She absolutely wanted to help me get the car out of the water and she said: 'But... what are you doing in the water without your bathing suit?' Oh the shame when she found out the answer..."

Basil, 25, single, London

AT A FANCY COCKTAIL PARTY

You are dressed up to the nines (tens even!) She looks radiant in her pretty dress and jewels. You are both looking fabulous and you both know it. However, what you would find even more fabulous would be a toilet posthaste!

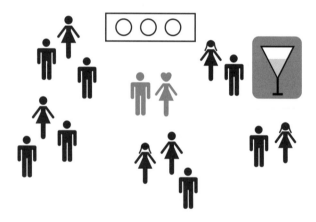

DIFFICULTY

SOLUTION: THE COCKTAIL GOLDEN RULES

1. This one's simple. Slip away from her using the method you've probably already used to get rid of other guests at the party, the ones you have already talked to.
2. Excuse yourself by using one of following: "I'll just pop for a refill.", "I'm going to pick up some petit-fours." or "Excuse me, I must have a word with..."
3. Sneak off to the toilet discreetly (INVISIBILITY rule).
4. After you have done your deed, don't come back. This is how it's done at cocktail parties.
5. Make sure nobody sees you leaving the toilet.
6. At the end of the cocktail party, send her a text telling her that you were looking for her everywhere but couldn't find her!

EXPERT'S OPINION

"Honestly, who has ever talked to the same person twice at a cocktail party? Except the waiter..."

TESTIMONIAL

"I had no trouble getting rid of her, but I found her ... in the line for the toilet. Apparently, the smoked salmon on the bed of cabbage-stuffed mushrooms with coconut crème that a famous chef created for the evening didn't go down so well. There were at least 15 of us squirming and jumping in the line for the toilet!"

Casper, 36, in a relationship, London

You are with her at a concert of her favourite singer. Just when their most famous song comes on, the need to poo comes over you as well...

DIFFICULTY

★ ★ ★ ★ ★

SOLUTION: THE NEWEST FAN

1. Yell: "Woohoo, I love this song!!! (In other words, do like everybody else.)
2. Jump up and down hysterically while screaming the name of the artist. (Here, too, do like everybody else, but – considering the state you're in – restrain yourself somewhat.)
3. Climb on the shoulders of a bloke standing next to you and crowd surf.
4. Do your absolute best to hold it in. Do not poo now.
5. As the crowd is carrying you, give directions (reminder: you want to go to the toilet): "Heeeh to the left, hooohoooh to the right!"
6. When the crowd puts you back down, go to the toilet.
7. Do your deed (you needn't worry about making inappropriate noises here; the concert will drown it out so go for it!)
8. At the end of the concert, tell your date: "I had no idea that a Barry Manilow concert could be such a madhouse!"

EXPERT'S OPINION

"This method is completely useless! Do you really think that you can hold it in while hundreds of people are pressing on your abdominal area?"

TESTIMONIAL

"I tried crowd surfing once, but I was at the opera, so everyone was sitting."
Bob, 32, married, Northampton

AT THE CINEMA

After buying everything you'll need to not go hungry during the film (a bucket of popcorn, an ice cream and an XXL beverage), you take your seat. She is leaning on you, eagerly awaiting the film. You are suddenly eager to go to the toilet...

DIFFICULTY

★ ★ ★ ★ ★

SOLUTION: BLACK NINJA

1. Wait for the film to begin and for the theatre to go dark.
2. Look around and find the darkest corner of the theatre.
3. Tell her you can't find your phone, and that you must have dropped it on your way in
4. Get up and pretend you're looking for it.
5. Now go to the dark corner that you noticed earlier.
6. Do your deed there while watching the film.
7. Wipe with your ticket.
8. Return to your seat.

EXPERT'S OPINION

"This kind of situation should never arise. Every normal human being knows his schedule and should never agree to go to the cinema at the time when he is usually, well, otherwise engaged."

TESTIMONIAL

"I carefully made it to the darkest part of the room, but once I was there and at it, a scene with a sunrise came on and lit up the whole room. The projection was immediately stopped and I was savagely escorted from the theatre, half naked."

Colin, 33, single, Stratford-upon-Avon

PLAYING GOLF

She wants to make you discover one of her passions: golf. The weather is nice, it's warm, the sun is shining... an idyllic day. She loves sharing what she loves, but for you the urge to go to the toilet grows with each wretched hole. There's no way you will make it to 18; you can barely walk.

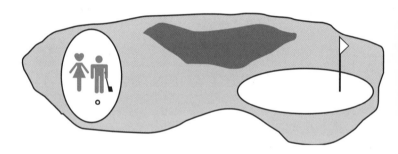

DIFFICULTY

SOLUTION: THE SAND TRAP

1. Position your golf ball on the tee (try not to tremble, despite the pain), hit the ball and make a deliberate bunker shot (into the sand).
2. Go to the bunker by yourself (INTIMACY rule).
3. Hunker down in the most hidden part of it and do your deed.
4. Once you're finished, put your clothes back on in the same manner as you had them before (IDENTITY rule) and cover up your deed with sand.
5. Rejoin the game.

EXPERT'S OPINION

"There are never enough toilets at golf courses. I know many people who quit the game just because they had to finish one too many rounds by desperately limping to the club house toilet."

TESTIMONIAL

"I followed this method exactly as described. I thought I'd done well, but then I realized that behind the bunker there was… the club restaurant. I will spare you the details; let's just say I am no longer welcome there. My fiancée still doesn't understand why I was banned from the club."

Charles, engaged, 34, Brighton

AT A RESTAURANT

You are at a restaurant. You were just served the aperitif: champagne with blackcurrant liquor. You quickly learn the powerful laxative effects of blackcurrant... In short: you must go to the toilet immediately, but you can't leave because she will know where you're headed. The best solution would be to not eat and to shorten the dinner.

DIFFICULTY

SOLUTION: JUST LIKE THE CANTEEN

1. Don't show any signs of pain or impatience (COMPOSURE rule). You must stay in seduction mode; don't ever show any signs of the 'mission: toilet' mode.
2. Do as you did when you were little and spread your food around the plate to make it seem as if you'd already eaten quite a bit of it.
3. Make her look away by saying that Brad Pitt has just entered the restaurant.
4. While she's looking, take her plate and empty half of it. (Put her steak in your pocket, her side dish in the champagne bucket and her vegetables under the table. Be inventive!)
5. When she finishes her food, tell her that the restaurant is following the latest trend and doesn't do desserts.
6. Like a proper gentleman, get up and pay at the bar. Take advantage of this absence to go and quickly do your deed.

EXPERT'S OPINION

"Speaking of celebrities, I offer an exclusive workshop on how to do your deed outdoors safe from the paparazzi. It helps them avoid gossip magazine covers with titles such as: 'George Clooney: painful diarrhoea ru[i]ns his holiday!'"

TESTIMONIAL

"I used this method, but the waiter came right after to serve us more champagne. I had to make a scene about the steak and vegetables in the champagne bucket."

Bill, 30, married, Leeds

AT THE THEATRE

You go to the theatre together. The so-called comedy you're watching is so bad it's making you want to poo violently, but the interval is still a long way away.

DIFFICULTY

SOLUTION: HIGHER GROUND

1. Sigh with desperation at the end of each tirade.
2. Turn to her and whisper into her ear: "This play is really bad... I will go around and explore this beautiful old theatre."
3. Climb up the stairs to one of the balconies that are still empty.
4. Hide behind the balustrade and do your deed without grimacing, while continuing to watch the play. (Your ticket was no doubt expensive; it would be a shame not to be able to watch for the next two hours.)
5. Once finished, hide your deed under a programme (SECURITY rule) and regain your seat without a word.

EXPERT'S OPINION

"There's nothing new about this method. It was used in the 15th century. The theatres smelled very badly back then so everyone got away with it."

TESTIMONIAL

"It was a Shakespeare play. A new actor came on the stage with a long piece of toilet paper stuck to his shoe. The whole theatre was cracking up. As for the actor, he was completely baffled as to how his tragic monologue was provoking so much laughter. I've never laughed so hard at the theatre in my life!"

Dennis, 35, engaged, Woking

A WALK IN THE FOREST

You suggested a walk in the forest. After 30 minutes of walking, you are far away from everything. She is enjoying the calm of the forest, but you keep looking at the leaves with sinister intentions...

DIFFICULTY

★ ★ ★ ★ ★

SOLUTION: EVOLUTIONARY THEORY

1. Don't tell her what you want to do (SECRECY rule) and let her walk slightly ahead of you.
2. Hide behind a thick bush where she can't see you.
3. Do your deed as quickly as possible.
4. Wipe with the leaves. (Again: the leaves of certain plant species can cause painful irritation that doesn't go away for days. Holly should only be used if there is absolutely nothing else available.)
5. Emerge from behind the bush with a big piece of wood, or interesting leaf species, so that she will think that was what you were looking for all that time.

EXPERT'S OPINION

"Relieving yourself in the woods allows one to reconnect with nature and it brings out the prehistoric man that lies dormant in all of us. Do it as often as possible; you will feel more connected to your environment and participate in the regeneration of the forest. Poo in the woods: it's one of the best things you can do for the environment!"

TESTIMONIAL

"I followed this method by the book. Just as I was in middle of it, a wild boar in heat came charging at me."
Anthony, 33, single, Oxford

You want to raise the heat between the two of you, and suggest going to the spa. Once in the sauna together, your temperature may be rising, but something else is ready to drop. This might be a good time to check for exits...

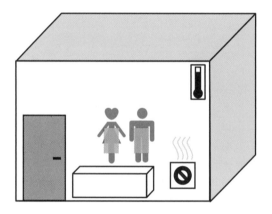

SOLUTION: CLAM BAKE

1. Tell her that you will put some more water on the stones in the sauna.
2. Get up and go towards the hot stones.
3. As she dozes off in the heat, do your deed discreetly in the furnace. You'll find the heat off the stones will immediately incinerate all traces of what you have just produced.
4. Before she notices the strange odour, say: "Ah, it smells of reindeer in this sauna! Just like in Finland. Now this is what I call a sauna!"

EXPERT'S OPINION

"I never go to a sauna anymore for precisely this reason, I just go to thermal spas."

TESTIMONIAL

"We were in Finland, and I used this method, but I burned my bum. At the hospital I told them that I burned it on the radiator in our hotel room. The doctor said to his colleague: 'Igmar, vielä sellaisen, joka on paska, joka saunankiuas, lähdin te.' I know some Finnish – it means: "Igmar, we have another one who pooed in the sauna. I'll let you deal with him.'"

Edward, in a relationship, 38, Bath

IN A LOUNGE BAR

You are in a lounge bar together. Cosy atmosphere, smooth music, dimmed lighting. You are deep in conversation, and she is already undressing you with her eyes, giving you hope for the rest of the night. Suddenly, the only thing you hope for is a WC.

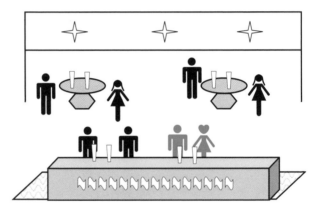

DIFFICULTY

SOLUTION: THE MOLE

1. Tell her that there are many pretty girls in this bar. You can be sure she will take a moment to scan the place.
2. With her attention elsewhere, tell the bartender: "I think the girl I'm talking to is a prostitute! She is making obvious advances at me, her dress is much too short, and she's just asked me how much money I had on me... Could you ask your bouncer to help me?"
3. Wait 30 seconds. Smile adoringly at her, rather than grimace in pain that you are no doubt feeling by now.
4. Watch her being escorted out by the bouncer. Look completely shocked by it.
5. Go to the toilet and relieve yourself.
6. Find her outside and ask her with an appropriate degree of shock and surprise: "What on Earth just happened?

EXPERT'S OPINION

"While you're at it, ask the bouncer to watch your toilet door during your time in there. You'll be more at ease."

TESTIMONIAL

"I tried to do it discreetly behind the speakers. It was I who was escorted from the bar…"

Alan, 31, single, Birmingham

AT A CLUB

You are at a club. The music is really good and your date is impressed with your John Travolta style moves. You are ready to dance the night away. Alas, suddenly the only thing you want to do is boogie towards the nearest toilet...

DIFFICULTY

SOLUTION: THE ALTERCATION

1. Keep dancing and identify the most menacing-looking bloke dancing close by.
2. Provoke him verbally. You have to make him want to hit you.
3. Tell him to come with you to the toilet to get this sorted.
4. Once you are there and you are sure your date can't see you, don't fight! Negotiate with the bloke and offer to buy him a drink to appease him.
5. Do your deed.
6. Return to your date and tell her that you really showed him!

EXPERT'S OPINION

"Make sure she doesn't see you buying the chap a drink. It might make her suspect you were hitting on him!"

TESTIMONIAL

"When we arrived at the toilet, I started to ask him not to beat me up and offer him a beer, when he offered to buy me a drink! It was incredible: he was applying this book's method and was looking for someone to fight with to go to the toilet. We instantly bonded, but only for a few moments – we then noticed that there was only one toilet available and we fought over who would go in there first."

Jeremy, 32, married, Newport

ON TOP OF THE EIFFEL TOWER

During a romantic weekend in Paris you decide to go all the way to the top of the Eiffel Tower. She loves this classic Parisian experience. You are trying to enjoy it with her, but on the inside you are screaming: "Where are the bloody toilets in this thing?"

DIFFICULTY

SOLUTION: THE FRIENDLY PHOTOGRAPHER

1. Find a group of at least ten Japanese tourists.
2. Suggest you take a picture of them so that they will have a great memory of their visit.
3. Give the camera to your girlfriend and arrange the Japanese in front of the barrier (important: make them squeeze closely together).
4. While she is busy setting the camera and struggling with its menu entirely in Japanese, slide to the very back of the group.
5. Take advantage of the human barrier in front of you to quickly do your deed (SECRECY and SPEED rules combined).
6. If you need more time, stand up (with your pants down), poke your head in between two of the Japanese tourists and tell your girlfriend: "Do another one, it's not every day they are in Paris!" Then go back to your business.

EXPERT'S OPINION

"My husband is a specialist in high altitude toilets in famous buildings. Recently he designed the toilets for the Burj Dubai tower: the toilet seats are solid gold and they flush with champagne!"

TESTIMONIAL

"There were no Japanese. I found some Chinese tourists, arranged them and proceeded to relieve myself. One of them saw me doing it and yelled something like: "Long pi luu wong!!!" I don't know what that means, but they all gathered around me to make a safety barrier. The Chinese really are fans of great walls!"

David, 32, married, Doncaster

ROLLERBLADING

You go rollerblading together, hand in hand. After 30 minutes you are overcome with an emergency – its time to locate the toilet...

DIFFICULTY

★★★★★

SOLUTION: THE GOOD OLD GAME

1. Suggest you play hide-and-seek on rollerblades.
2. Explain what this game is.
3. Tell her: "1: cover your eyes and count to 3,600!"
4. As soon as she covers her eyes and starts counting loudly, you are free to go.
5. Take advantage of the entire hour she will be counting to find a comfortable toilet, buy a few magazines and do your deed while catching up on the news.
6. Don't forget to hide afterwards.

EXPERT'S OPINION

"A proctologist in London has confirmed to me that doing an hour of rollerblading has the same effect as taking five laxatives. Now when you see someone grimacing as he is rollerblading, you'll know that it is not the extreme effort but the extreme urge to go to the toilet that is causing such facial contortions!"

TESTIMONIAL

"I'm a bit of a daredevil, so I tried doing it by getting slightly behind her and crouching while continuing to rollerblade. It didn't work – I fell half naked just as the first bomb dropped. Result: a new dimension in skid-marks, a nasty scar on my bum and probably the biggest embarrassment of my life."

Kevin, 26, in a relationship nevertheless (!), Edinburgh

You are doing one of the world's most romantic activities together: ice skating. She loves holding your hand, but you would happily trade all the money in the world for white porcelain right now.

SOLUTION: THE TRIPLE LUTZ

1. Whatever your level, tell her you will give her a demonstration of figure skating.
2. Skate and wave your arms around madly.
3. Once you are sufficiently far from her, attempt a triple lutz, the goal being that you fall behind the barrier.
4. You now have 30 seconds to do your deed behind the barrier – the time it takes her to skate across the rink to check if you are alright. (Advice: stop the mad arm-waving while you're doing it.)
5. Get up quickly (SPEED rule) and return to the skating rink. If your legs feel somewhat constrained, you probably forgot to put your trousers on.

EXPERT'S OPINION

"I often compare figure skating in a relationship to an animal courtship: a mad young turkey trying to seduce a young peacock in a rut."

TESTIMONIAL

"Everything went smoothly, she didn't see me do it, but I was so focussed on making it behind the barrier that I didn't notice there were dozens of people seated in the bleachers. They got their money's worth..."

Nelson, 56, single, London

AT THE SPA

You are at a thermal spa and enjoying all the activities together. All that iodine in the air is giving you a strong urge to go to the toilet, but she is constantly next to you everywhere you go. It's impossible to escape.

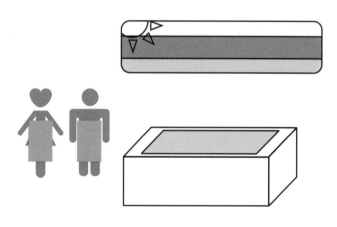

DIFFICULTY

SOLUTION: A NEW ACTIVITY

1. Tell her that you saw in the brochure that they offer baths in sea mud, and that a friend told you it was fantastic.
2. Add: "The mud is heated to 39°. You'll love it!"
3. Once you are sitting in the mud bath, you know what you need to do.
4. Come out as soon as you've finished (SPEED rule) and look outraged.
5. Yell: "What is this smell? This isn't sea mud, that's poo that you put in this bath!"
6. Put your robe on and march indignantly to the director's office.
7. Describe what's happened to you and ask to be reimbursed for the whole week at the spa.

EXPERT'S OPINION

"This is just terrible!"

TESTIMONIAL

"I let her in on it, and now we do it all the time. We've already had eight weeks free at different thermal spas this year."

Paul, 32, married, London

JOGGING TOGETHER

It's spring. She is trying to lose the extra winter pounds and invites you to go jogging with her. As soon as you take off, you realize that it's the toilet that you'll have to run to very soon. You won't be able to wait much longer as each new step is pure torture.

DIFFICULTY

SOLUTION: THE RABBIT AND THE TURTLE

1. Keep running and look at her.
2. Say: "I think it would best if we took a break. You are completely red and I'm afraid you'll suffocate. Don't worry; you've already done a great job with all that fat you have to carry around."
3. Leave her there dumbstruck and run away.
4. As soon as you are far away enough, find a bush or bin and do your deed quickly (SPEED rule).
5. Come back to her as soon as possible (careful: don't show her that you, too, are completely out of breath), and say: "You look angry. Don't take personally what I said earlier, I was just talking about a proven scientific fact that women carry around more fat than men. It's genetics."

EXPERT'S OPINION

"Rule 1: Don't ever mention weight to a woman. I can't believe it! If you don't know that, you might as well tell her during a date: 'OK, I'm off because I have to make a deposit in the toilet bank.' You are a lost cause."

TESTIMONIAL

"Ever since I was little, it's happened every time with every sport: as soon as I would start moving, I had to go to the toilet within five minutes. I was mocked so much that I had to give up all group sports."

Philip, 34, single, Swansea

THE MASSAGE

She is giving you a massage with coconut oil. You are having a nice time together in this sensual activity. However, when she massages your belly, she stimulates your intestines and suddenly you simply must go to the toilet. You feel bad because now you can no longer fully appreciate her massage, but there is nothing you can do.

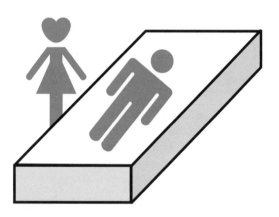

DIFFICULTY

SOLUTION: YOUR DOG

1. Start telling her the story of your dog Skip that you had when you were five.
2. Tell her how playful he was and how he made the whole family laugh. He was the kindest dog in the world.
3. Then, switching to a grave and more emotional tone, describe to her in detail how one day he sacrificed his life to save the life of Tony the three-legged hamster.
4. She will undoubtedly start crying and wipe her eyes with her hands, covered in coconut oil.
5. The coconut will irritate her eyes and she will have to go the bathroom to wash her eyes.
6. Use this time to sneak off to the toilet and do your deed as quickly as possible (SPEED rule). Be careful not to slip; don't forget you are as slick as a baby seal with all that coconut oil.
7. Go back and put yourself in the same position you were in when she left (IDENTITY rule).
8. Resume the activity as if nothing happened (SILENCE rule).

EXPERT'S OPINION

"Massage is a great activity to do together, but always avoid the stomach! It is not a coincidence that massage salons only offer back massages!"

TESTIMONIAL

"She knew nothing about massages. Every time she pressed on my stomach, I farted. It was the worst half hour of my life! I think hers, too. We've never done it since." Peter, 49, married, Birmingham

PART 2: AT HER PLACE

How do you operate in unfamiliar terrain when the need arises?

You are at her place and you have some trouble adapting to this hostile environment. Is there ever a way to deal with toilet overflow and nearly flooding her place? What do you do when there is no more toilet paper? You can't call for help! Worse yet, what do you do when you get stuck in the toilet? In this part of the book, we will give you concrete solutions to avoid any faux pas while you are miles away from your comfort zone.

She insists on introducing you to her cat. You know this cat means a lot to her, so you agree to go to her flat. But what you really want is to meet her toilet.

DIFFICULTY

★ ★ ★ ★ ★

SOLUTION: ON ALL FOURS

1. By no means tell her that the only reason you accepted her invitation was to be able to relieve yourself (SECRECY rule).
2. After a few minutes, try to distract her. Depending on her geographic location in the flat, decide what's best: to do it discreetly and quickly in the toilet without her noticing or use her cat's litter tray. If you choose the latter, don't forget to apply the SECURITY rule and cover up your poo.
3. Never bring up the cat toilet feat (MODESTY rule).

EXPERT'S OPINION

"Since we are talking about domestic animals, I would take this opportunity to warn you never to do it in a dog house. You risk getting stuck in such a cramped space, not to mention appearing in a local newspaper, and then in 7,564 articles on the internet translated into 34 different world languages."

TESTIMONIAL

"I applied this method. It smelled awful so she said she needed to clean the cat's litter. She didn't say anything when she came back, but I could see that she couldn't understand how her kitty could have produced something quite so enormous."

George, 45, a hardened singleton, Bolton

SHE CONFIDES IN YOU

You are spending the evening at her place. Since you know that you must appear interested and a good listener, you ask her plenty of questions about her life. She starts telling you a story about an episode in her life that was obviously very important to her, when suddenly you feel an uncontrollable urge to go to the toilet. It would be very, very bad to interrupt her, but you just can't hold it in anymore.

DIFFICULTY

SOLUTION: THE SACRED DOOR

1. Tell her that you have read about a revolutionary method in a psychology magazine on how to liberate yourself from the weight of your past. To do it, one must a) not see their confidant, and b) isolate oneself from all external noise.
2. Suggest you try it by symbolically using the toilet door between you.
3. Take a pencil and go into the toilet.
4. Slide a piece of toilet paper under the door on which you wrote: 'I am listening.'
5. While she is telling you her terrible secret and crying, do your deed. From time to time slide pieces of toilet paper on which you wrote 'Yes', 'I understand', 'That's terrible'.
6. Wait for her to finish before coming out, and then gather all the pieces of toilet paper from the floor.
7. Throw them into the toilet and flush to symbolize the pain that is leaving her.

EXPERT'S OPINION

"An essential piece of advice: don't pass all of the toilet paper under the door."

TESTIMONIAL

"I didn't lock the door behind me so she wouldn't find it suspicious. She didn't like the method and opened the door at the worst possible moment…"

John, 52, single, York

YOU BREAK THE TOILET SEAT

You said you were going to "wash your hands" as a cover up, but this time the toilet seat actually broke while you were doing the deed. The situation is very awkward, as she will soon find out that you ruined her toilet. It won't give you any brownie points in her book!

DIFFICULTY

★★★★★

SOLUTION: NEW TOILET SEAT

1. Put the toilet lid down.
2. Kick in the centre of the lid to break only the middle of it.
   This is the first step in making a new toilet seat.
3. Finish it off with your car key functioning as a knife, and use her nail file to smooth off the edges (be diligent here to prevent any shards getting stuck in the next user's bum).
4. Take off the broken toilet seat.
5. Leave the toilet holding the broken toilet seat hidden behind your back. (Piece of advice: slide it under your shirt and stand upright.)
6. Tell her you need to get up early in the morning and leave immediately.

EXPERT'S OPINION

"Not putting down the toilet seat is the cause of one in three divorces in the USA."

TESTIMONIAL

"I haven't broken the toilet seat at her place. However, she has already broken mine! I don't understand how she could possibly have done it. Maybe she was jumping up and down in order to shake it out of her?"

Axel, 42, in a relationship for the moment, Carmarthen

THE TOILET OVERFLOWS

You found an innocent pretext to go to the toilet. When you finish, you flush as discreetly as possible... but the water won't stop running and the toilet overflows. The situation is very dramatic and the water – and everything else – soon runs under the door...

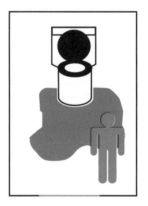

DIFFICULTY

SOLUTION: THE GOOD DEED

1. To stop the flood, close the pipe that feeds the toilet flush.
2. Leave the toilet carefully without her noticing you (INVISIBILITY rule).
3. Find a mop, a bucket and a cleaning product.
4. Clean the corridor using the water that came from the toilet.
   Make a lot of noise. You want her to come see what's going on.
5. When she sees you cleaning, she will tell herself that you are not
   like all the other men who never pitch in with household chores.

EXPERT'S OPINION

"If you have enough toilet paper available, find refuge on the toilet seat and from there throw toilet paper all around you. The powerful absorption capacity of toilet paper will do miracles. Gather it all up with the toilet brush or use the lid of the air freshener as a little shovel."

TESTIMONIAL

"I've never had this problem, but I've had another very similar one at her place. She has an automatic flush. Every time I go, I manage to set it off at least six or seven times while I'm in there. I'm sure she thinks I'm trying to flush something enormous..."

Benjamin, 37, in a relationship, Cardiff

NO PAPER

You told her you were going to use her bathroom to wash your hands. When you do your deed, you realize that there is no toilet paper. You risk exposing your false pretenses...but also need to locate a decent wiping device.

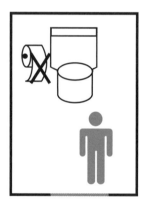

DIFFICULTY

★ ★ ★ ★ ★

SOLUTION: DIY

1. Stay calm (SECURITY and SILENCE rules combined)
2. Unscrew the radiator from the bathroom wall. Remove the wallpaper from behind the radiator. (Be careful: don't go beyond the limits of the radiator's position, and make sure the strips are big enough.)
3. Use the wallpaper as toilet paper.
4. Screw the radiator back on.

EXPERT'S OPINION

"I recommend you always carry a spanner or two when visiting the toilet. And since we're on the subject of DIY, let me mention my online course: 'How to unblock the toilet with your car keys.'"

TESTIMONIAL

"I used this method two years ago and I loved the softness of the wallpaper. From then on I bought discontinued wallpaper at a nearby DIY shop. However, the shop owner is starting to give me funny looks. In a year I bought enough wallpaper to cover a huge house with nothing but scraps. He must think I have really crap taste."

Steven, 38, married, Inverness

THE TERRIBLE SMELL

You were overcome by a vicious desire to go to the toilet. You managed to distract her for a few minutes to do your deed. You got everything right, but you didn't count on a nauseatingly bad odour now coming out of the toilet and slowly spreading throughout her flat.

DIFFICULTY

SOLUTION: THE CHANEL TECHNIQUE

1. Quickly find a bottle of perfume and spray yourself with it. Use generously.
2. Find her and embrace her, holding her close to you.
3. Wait until the odour dissipates.
4. Let go only when the air is decontaminated.

EXPERT'S OPINION

"Certain odours are so tenacious that even emptying a bottle of perfume will not mask them. This is a problem of which the engineers working on toilet air fresheners are well aware. The leading companies in this field spend between 38 and 52 million dollars in research to find a way to eliminate these smelly particles that are internally referred to as P4 or 'Particularly Putrid Persistent Particles'. This is a very promising market, as the P4's are produced by around 10–15% of the population, and as yet, there is no solution on the market for these poor souls."

TESTIMONIAL

"I am one of the P4 people. I've done everything and spared no expense to try and do something about it. I bought state-of-the-art German equipment powerful enough to air a 56m^2 room in eight seconds. My toilet only measures 10m^2. I had to find a way to secure the toilet paper so it doesn't get sucked out. However, this brought on another problem: my neighbours are complaining to the authorities about foul odours emanating from my ventilation system."

James, 30, single, Peterborough

YOU ARE STUCK IN THE TOILET

You go to the toilet under the ruse that you need to go and look for something that you left in the pocket of your coat hanging in the hallway. Once your deed is done, the key breaks in the lock and you can't get out. You panic.

DIFFICULTY

SOLUTION: THE BREAK

1. Take off the top of the toilet flush and use it to break the toilet door.
2. Once the door is in tatters, go out stealthily.
3. She will come to see what all the noise is about. Explain that you caught a burglar breaking the toilet door.
4. Raise your voice and ask, *CSI*-style: "Would you happen to have an ex boyfriend who is mad at you and wanted to take it out on your toilet?"
5. Let her suggest possible reasons.

EXPERT'S OPINION

"Let me share a personal anecdote. This has already happened to me. I tried to go out by the toilet window but I got stuck... I had to call the fire brigade. I will not say anything further about this misadventure."

TESTIMONIAL

"I wasn't familiar with this technique. I called for help. It took three hours to pick the lock. When I came out, her father, her uncle, her mother and four neighbours were standing at the door. She'd called them all for help. Ever since then they've been using the nickname "Toilet-Man" for me. Go to hell. It happened over six years ago."

Alastair, 32, married, Glasgow

YOU ARE COOKING TOGETHER

You are in her kitchen, all set to impress her with your favourite dish. The fear of not succeeding is giving you knots in your stomach, which turns into a desperate need to go to the toilet.

DIFFICULTY

SOLUTION: THE UPSIDE DOWN SOUFFLÉ

1. Stay calm (COMPOSURE rule). Tell her that your specialty is the upside down soufflé and that each time you make it, everybody licks the plate.
2. Take two eggs and whisk them in a bowl.
3. Add half a crispbread and put everything in the oven.
4. Ask her to watch the dish carefully and take it out as soon as the mix explodes like popcorn and spins around in the bowl.
5. Sit her on a chair in front of the oven and sneak off to the toilet to do your deed (INVISIBILITY rule).
6. Upon your return, ask her if the soufflé has done what it was supposed to. She will tell you that it didn't.
7. Don't hesitate to make her feel guilty. Show her that it's her fault that your specialty didn't work out, and that the evening you had planned is now ruined. She will try to make it up to you, which can end up being a very good thing for you.

EXPERT'S OPINION

"Speaking of food: I know that my clients always ask themselves after examining their stools: 'When did I eat corn?'"

TESTIMONIAL

"I am regularly constipated, so when I go to the toilet at her place, it's always difficult. I need a small bench under my feet while I toil away. Lifting up my legs puts my intestines in a more favourable position, according to my doctor. Therefore I always have to sneak away with a small red chair from her living room, go to the toilet unnoticed, and put the chair back, also unnoticed. It's a mission worthy of special forces, all while suffering excrutiating stomach pain." Eric, 29, in a relationship, Dublin

THE DOOR DOESN'T CLOSE

You are in the toilet, but the door won't close. She might walk in on you while you're mid-deed in her toilet. The relationship will be over when that happens.

DIFFICULTY

SOLUTION: A CULT SERIES

1. Take a roll of white toilet paper (it must be white, otherwise this method won't work).
2. Wrap the paper around your head. Cover up your whole head, including your face and hair.
3. Now that you have become the Invisible Man, she won't be able to see you if she enters the toilet.

   However, stay vigilant. Even though you are the Invisible Man, you can still be smelled and touched. If she enters, stand by the wall.

EXPERT'S OPINION

"Ah, the heroes from TV shows; so often they become a source of fantasies. Play the role of your partner's favourite character and your relationship will last. Personally I often dress up as Xena the warrior princess."

TESTIMONIAL

"I used the method of levitation that I read about in your other book, *How To Poo At Work*. I was two meters above ground. She entered the toilet, groaned that someone forgot to flush, and did what she came in to do. She was completely oblivious to the fact that I was levitating one meter above her. I then finished what I was doing."

Max, 42, married, Manchester

PART 3: AT YOUR PLACE

What do you do when a certain need arises, but you are not by yourself in your flat?

Don't be fooled: just because you are in a familiar environment, it doesn't mean that the situation is not extremely dangerous. If she is at your place, you can't leave the toilet door open as you usually do in order to be able to watch the TV in the living room at the same time. Not to mention catching up on your phone messages, calling your mum and other tasks that you usually take care of while taking care of business. Luckily for you, the golden rules still apply! Find out how here...

A WEBCAM CHAT

You are enjoying a webcam chat together, so although she is not physically in your apartment, she is certainly in your space. While she is LOLing and ROTFLing at all the funny things you are saying, disaster strikes and you are suddenly taken with the need to go to the toilet....

DIFFICULTY

SOLUTION: THE X-RATED SOLUTION

1. Tell her that you've always fantasized about her doing a striptease for you via webcam.
2. Tell her that you will shut down your webcam so that she will feel more at ease and less inhibited.
3. Go and perform your deed while she performs hers.
4. When you come back, turn your webcam back on and tell her it was fantastic.
5. Continue the conversation (SILENCE rule).

EXPERT'S OPINION

"E-sex, e-chats... everything is becoming virtual, there are even e-fights! Some day we will even have e-children adopted in another part of the world and raise them via webcam!"

TESTIMONIAL

"I have a laptop with an integrated camera. I didn't want to miss the striptease so I took the computer with me to the toilet. Sadly I touched the wrong button and my camera stayed on… She didn't much appreciate my striptease."

Gerry, 38, single, Aberdeen

SHE WANTS YOU TO DRIVE HER HOME

You've just spent a nice evening together and you sense that she would like you to drive her home. You are already fighting the urge to go to the toilet, so the journey will feel very, very, long indeed. Unless...

DIFFICULTY

SOLUTION: DRUNK IN CHARGE

1. Grab your car keys and start telling her how you bought your driving license for only 12 Euro in Bosnia.
2. Slip into the conversation that yesterday someone stole your windscreen.
3. Keep chatting with her and pour yourself 'one for the road': a double whisky, followed by a triple vodka, straight.
4. As soon as the alcohol is visibly having an effect on you, suggest that you take her home. Tell her that even though it's pouring down, you should be ok with a good anorak.
5. If you set the stage well, she will refuse and opt to walk, take a taxi or the bus.
6. Once she is gone, go to the toilet without any worries.

EXPERT'S OPINION

"It is well known that a mix of certain alcohols can have strong laxative effects. Be careful what you drink."

TESTIMONIAL

"I am not a big drinker and I could only find an old bottle of schnapps that some German family friends gave me. I had three big shots. I don't know what happened after that, but when I woke up I was violently ill and had to call an industrial cleaning company to clean my toilet..."

Ian, 29, single, Perth

YOU PLAY WII TOGETHER

You are at your house playing tennis on your Nintendo Wii. After an hour of back and forth, you are all shaken up and suddenly furious with the Japanese engineers who invented this physical way of playing video games: because of them you must really go to the toilet.

DIFFICULTY

SOLUTION: THE NEW RULES

1. Tell your friend that you are a member of the Wii-Club in your town and that you are ranked highly in Wii-Tennis, almost a professional.
2. Claim that you can beat her with your eyes closed.
3. She will take your word for it and accept the challenge.
4. Just as you close your eyes, tell her: "Wait, I'll go and stay in the toilet so you can't accuse me of peeking later!"
5. Once you are in the toilet, take off your pants and sit down. Ask her to turn up the volume so that you can play by sound (this will help you cover up any flatulence).
6. While doing your deed, flail the nunchuk around to try to score points.
7. Once the game is over, come back and tell her (if you didn't win, of course, which is the most likely outcome): "You are better than I thought!"

EXPERT'S OPINION

"I called Nintendo. The warranty department confirmed to me that they receive between 45–60 calls every day about nunchuks that were dropped in the toilet. They researched this phenomenon. The clients in question are those who have installed a Wii and a screen in their toilets."

TESTIMONIAL

"We weren't playing tennis, but rather a dumb game in which you have to tap the coconuts on both sides as fast as possible. I told her I was so good at it I could beat her from the toilet. When there, I had a brilliant idea: I strapped the nunchuk to the toilet seat by wrapping it tightly with toilet paper. Thanks to the handle of the lid, I beat the world record of the game. I was contacted by Nintendo, and I am leaving tomorrow for Japan as a contestant in a world championship, with a toilet seat in my suitcase of course.

Damian, 26, in a relationship, Manchester

YOU WATCH A DVD

You are watching a romantic film together. She is having a wonderful time and wants this moment to last forever. You need it to end as soon as possible so that you can go to the toilet.

SOLUTION: WAR OF THE NERVES

1. Go and make some popcorn.
2. Come back to the couch and chew your popcorn very loudly (to get the desired effect, imagine you are a wild boar eating a big bucket of corn).
3. Get up and bring back a beer for yourself. Ask her if she wants a drink too, but then forget to bring it to her.
4. Then change positions on the couch at least five times in less than a minute.
5. Turn on a lamp next to the TV. Thirty seconds later, turn it off.
6. Now take the remote and randomly turn the volume up and down.
7. By now she should be getting really annoyed.
8. Make idiotic predictions for the end of the film and say things like: "Oh, I know this actor, he was in... Oh , I don't remember the name... You know, that American TV series." Carry on until she can't take it anymore.
9. With her at the end of her nerves, she will tell you that she needs to get up early and leave. You can then finally go to the toilet.

EXPERT'S OPINION

"If the film is scary and she is trying to get in your arms for you to calm her, take advantage of this proximity and stuff popcorn in her ears. That will really get her mad!"

TESTIMONIAL

"We were watching *Titanic*. After an hour I couldn't take it anymore. I just had to go to the toilet. I couldn't go through the whole list so I went straight for the jugular: I told her that the ship sinks at the end. She was furious and yelled: 'Why did you have to tell me how it ends!?' She went back to her place, fuming." Vincent, 29, single, London

SHE WILL BE THERE ANY MINUTE

You are at your place. She rings the intercom of your building. As you are about to open the door for her, you are taken with an urgent need to poo. You only have the time it will take her to get up to your floor to do your deed. And that's clearly not enough time.

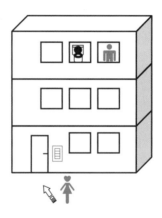

DIFFICULTY

★★★★★

SOLUTION: THE LOUSY REPAIRMAN

1. Don't panic (COMPOSURE rule).
2. As soon as you buzz her in, call and then block the lift on your floor. Use an object from your flat to do that, such as a chair, a kitchen appliance etc. That way she will wait a while downstairs, and then decide to walk up, which will buy you some time.
3. Go and speedily do your deed. (Ultra SPEED rule).
4. Unblock the lift.

EXPERT'S OPINION

"I remember a patient who was a psychopathic fetichist and who had to do his deed in a different lift every day. The local newspapers nicknamed him 'The Lift Whiffer' because he was spreading his little turds all over town. I had him locked up in a maximum security institution for the worst mental disorders."

TESTIMONIAL

"After I went, the smell was atrocious. I panicked and emptied the whole bottle of air freshener in the air. When she arrived the flat smelled strongly of pine. She made it seem like she didn't notice, but we both knew that the other knew."

Andre, 37, in a relationship, Leicester

SHE WANTS TO COME UP

Your date is about to end. Everything went really well, but then she lingers at your door and wants to come up. You would love nothing more than a night-cap, but right at that moment your priority is to run screaming into your toilet...

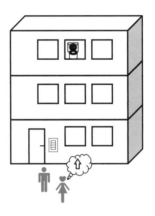

DIFFICULTY

★ ★ ★ ★ ★

SOLUTION: SPELEOLOGY

1. By no means show that you have to go to the toilet (SECRECY rule).
2. As you enter your apartment, don't turn on the light but whisper: "Take off your shoes and don't make any noise or you'll wake up my father, my grandmother, my uncle and my great grandmother who are sleeping in our living room." She should be a tad surprised.
3. Tell her: "Times are difficult. We decided to all live together in my place to reduce our living expenses."
4. If she hasn't turned around yet, add: "Keep your coat with you because you can use it as a pillow. The kitchen floor is not very comfortable, even with the towel I will give you to lie on."
5. Add to that: "OK, I will go now. I sleep with Nana."
6. By now, she must have run out. You can go to the toilet in peace.
7. As soon as you have finished, text her to tell her it was just a joke (it's very funny) and ask her to come back.

EXPERT'S OPINION

"Just so you know, I give free three-week sessions to anyone who slept for several years in the same bed as their grandmother. Contact me at my office."

TESTIMONIAL

"Relieved to hear my story, she told me that she too was living with her great great grandmother aged 108, her 27 uncles and aunts and 39 cousins. I didn't know how to respond to that, so I just blurted: 'Go home, I have to take a dump!'"

Emmanuel, 30, single, Exeter

PART 4: TOP LOVE

How do you handle poo urges when the physical attraction is at its climax?

You want to make love and you need to go to the toilet? You will be surprised to learn that you can manage both of these seemingly incompatible physiological needs simultaneously, by strictly following certain rules of course. In this chaper we address all the situations that could arise when we are in love and the desire to poo is at its peak...but which one comes first?

YOU ARE ABOUT TO KISS HER

You spent an evening together and the sexual tension between the two of you is palpable. You are about to kiss her. You really want her, but in your head all you are thinking about is the delight of squeezing out a huge poo...

DIFFICULTY

★ ★ ★ ★ ★

SOLUTION: MY LITTLE PONY

1. Lovingly approach her mouth with yours.
2. Just as she thinks you are going to kiss her, ask her if by any chance she's just had the Moldavian specialty, pony with onions.
3. She will run to the bathroom to brush her teeth.
4. Take advantage of this for a quick poo (SPEED rule). Hopefully she follows the British Dental Association recommendations for oral health and brushes for three minutes at least.
5. When she comes back, passionately kiss her.

EXPERT'S OPINION

"Another question that works just as well: 'Did you just eat seal lard with garlic?'"

TESTIMONIAL

"She had a ceasar salad for lunch. I could identify lettuce, bread and anchovies in her teeth. It wasn't a bad idea for her to go brush her teeth anyway."
Paul, 26, single, Headington

BEFORE YOU MAKE LOVE

Finally! The moment you've been waiting for has arrived. You are about to make love! Just as she unbuttons your trousers, you feel the need to decorate the toilet in the worst possible way. Your special moment is about to be ruined. Or is it?

DIFFICULTY

SOLUTION: THE KINBAKU

1. Whisper in her ear that you would like to try some light bondage and ask if she has a rope to tie you up with.
2. Since you are about to fulfil a *50 Shades of Grey* fantasy, she'll be game, but probably won't have any rope.
3. Ask her to wait in bed for a few minutes because you've just had an idea.
4. Go to the toilet. Do it as fast as you can (SPEED rule).
5. Take a roll of toilet paper and start wrapping it around your body.
6. Let your imagination take hold of you. Try to make something pretty because bondage is first and foremost an artistic activity.
7. After a few minutes you will probably resemble a mummy.
8. Hop back to the bedroom (remember, your feet are bound by toilet paper) and say: "Well, I guess it doesn't look as good as I'd hoped, what do you think?"
9. Let her unwrap you and make love in the usual way.

EXPERT'S OPINION

"If her reaction is positive, suggest to your staff at work to do promotions dressed as mummies. It should work really well."

TESTIMONIAL

"Two days prior she told me that her favourite cartoon was the *Pink Panther*. So I used pink toilet paper to dress up. She loved it and has asked for it many times since."

Quentin, 37, married, Edinburgh

SHE TELLS YOU SHE LOVES YOU

The big moment is here: she tells you that she loves you. You love her too, but what you would love even more at that very moment is to drop a few pounds down by the waterside...

DIFFICULTY

SOLUTION: A GIFT FROM THE HEART

1. Tell her you love her too.
2. Ask her to close her eyes for three minutes so that you can go and look for a special gift for this special moment.
3. Tiptoe to the toilet (INVISIBILITY rule).
4. While you are doing your deed, grab the toilet brush and hold it turned upwards like a torch.
5. The idea is to transform the toilet brush into a magnificent exotic flower. To do that, place little bits of toilet paper in between the bristles, making them look like beautiful flower petals. The brush will serve as the centre of the flower.
6. To make it even more realistic, use the toilet air freshener and spray your flower with it liberally.
7. Don't make her wait too long (SPEED rule). She is no doubt impatient to see what her gift was. Come out carefully and present your exotic creation, telling her that you wanted to 'say it with flowers'.

EXPERT'S OPINION

"OK, I know love is blind, but I have some difficulty believing that she will take your toilet brush full of toilet paper and smelling, well, of toilet, as an exotic flower!"

TESTIMONIAL

"There were two brushes in the toilet so I could make a bouquet! The brushes were white, the paper was pink – it was magnificent!"

John, married, 42, Croydon

SHE SUGGESTS YOU TAKE A BATH TOGETHER

You are at her apartment. She announces that the bathtub is filled with hot water and that she would like to go in there to 'relax' with you. She slips into the water. What would relax you, first and foremost, is a long perch on the loo with a good magazine. Failing that...

DIFFICULTY

1. Tell her that it would be even more romantic with candles and that you will go and get some.
2. If the toilet is not in the bathroom, you can go and use it to relieve yourself.
3. If the toilet is in the same room as the bath, you will have to find an alternative solution. The kitchen sink is usually the best choice.
4. Once you've done your deed, help yourself to different utensils (knives, scissors, blender…) to make your poo disappear. Use a lot of water and don't spare the dish soap (you will need at least a pint or two to make the odour disappear).
5. Use paper napkins to dry the sink (IDENTITY rule).

EXPERT'S OPINION

"In such a situation never get into a hot bath! It has a strong laxative effect and you risk provoking an incident commonly known as the 'brown fish'."

TESTIMONIAL

"We were at her place. Her American-style kitchen sink had an integrated garbage disposal. Great, I thought, this will be easy! No luck: what I produced was too big and it blocked the garbage disposal. I didn't say anything. She called the plumber who quickly diagnosed the situation: 'Miss, the thing that is blocking your garbage disposal is an enormous turd.' His words are still echoing in my head. Unfortunately, she quickly identified the culprit."

Michael, 30, single, Brighton

You've just spent the night together. In the morning she wants to snuggle and just enjoy your company. But it's the morning, and your body works like clockwork: Wake up – time to poo!

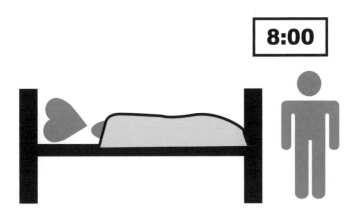

DIFFICULTY

★ ★ ★ ★ ★

SOLUTION: THE SAD TRUTH

1. Enjoy the softness of her skin for a few moments, despite the urgency.
2. Kiss her tenderly and say: "By any chance did you eat the pony with onions during the night again?" As she leaves to go brush her teeth, you can add: "Since you'll already be in the bathroom you can take a shower too while you're at it."
3. To compensate for any bad reaction (you never know), tell her that you will go and buy croissants while she's at it.
4. As soon as you hear the water running, grab your phone and run to the toilet (The INTIMACY and INVISIBILITY rule combo).
5. While you're doing your deed, send CROISSANTS to 08 12 34 (£9.75 per text – minimum 3 texts).
6. Come out of the toilet without leaving any trace of having been there (SECURITY and SPEED rule combo) and pick up the express delivery of croissants.
7. When she comes out, tell her that she smells nice and show her the breakfast that you lovingly prepared for her.

EXPERT'S OPINION

"Love also means accepting the morning breath of your partner. Nature made us all equal in this regard. If your partner always seems to have a minty breath in the morning it doesn't mean that he is wired differently, but rather that he got up before you to do his deed and brushed teeth at the same time."

TESTIMONIAL

"I must have typed the wrong number. I sent CROISSANTS to 08 12 33 and received a text telling me: 'Sorry, she's cheating on you. If you want to know if your girlfriend's new boyfriend likes your bum, send MOON to 08 98 76 – £8.24 per text." Samuel, 25, single, London

PART 5: EVERYDAY LIFE

Simple everyday situations can turn into a nightmare when we are overtaken by an uncontrollable urge to go to the toilet.

What do you do, for example, when you are on the tube together during rush hour and other passengers are constantly pressing against your belly and thus amplifying your anguish? What could help you when you stink up the only toilet at her parents' house, or break a lacquered wood toilet brush that was a family heirloom? And last but not least, how do you suffer through a stomach bug without her noticing? Find out all our solutions in the final chapter of this book.

ON THE PHONE

You are at your place and have been chatting for several minutes on the phone. Everything is going well, you are making her laugh, when suddenly a problem that is no laughing matter arises: you must go to the toilet immediately.

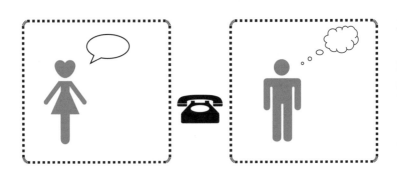

DIFFICULTY

SOLUTION: THE SAFETY BLANKET

1. Without changing the subject, go to the toilet and continue the conversation.
2. Sit down quietly (SECRECY rule).
3. Put your sweater on your thighs to cover up any errant noise that could reveal to her what you are doing.
4. Keep the door open in order to prevent the echo that anyone could recognize. (Your interlocutor is surely also guilty of having used the phone in the toilet from time to time.)
5. Wait until you hang up to flush.

EXPERT'S OPINION

"The statistics have confirmed it: the use of phones while in the toilet is going through the roof! In the 1980s it was considered marginal behaviour of only 0.02% of population. Since then, wireless and mobile phones have made it easier and this deviant behaviour is now popularized (yes, you read it right: deviant!). Phone makers are already adapting phone designs for this phenomenon: in 2015 all mobile phones will be equipped with a 'no toilet echo' function."

TESTIMONIAL

"In the 1980s, I got sick and tired of walking like a penguin in the hallway to answer the phone when it rang while I was, well, occupied. I was one of the first users of phones in the toilet: I bought a 12-meter extension for my phone so I could use it in there."

Thomas, 57, in a relationship, Manchester

You are at an important milestone: visiting her parents so that she can introduce you to them. You are having the first drink together when the need to go to the toilet comes over you.

DIFFICULTY

★ ★ ★ ★ ★

SOLUTION: THE SAVIOUR

1. Present yourself as an expert on carcinogenic household particles.
2. In the conversation about it, ask them what toilet air freshener brand they use (according to some studies, particles found in air fresheners are worse than cigarettes in causing lung cancer).
3. When they tell you their preferred brand, say that you are not familiar with it. Tell them that you'll go and check the list of ingredients on the bottle.
4. Go and fetch the air freshener bottle and use the trip to the toilet to quicky and discreetly do your deed.
5. Come back from the toilet, air freshener in hand, and tell them that theirs is among the most dangerous that are on the market. Tell them that you will get rid of it for them. (Free air freshener for you!)

EXPERT'S OPINION

"Another basic rule for visiting her parents: while it is perfectly normal that you panic when you stink up their toilet, never spray the air freshener more than twice in any given situation. Coming back smelling of 'Tropical Citrus Breeze' is not a good idea. Everybody will look at you just like in school when you came back from the loo and entered the classroom."

TESTIMONIAL

"I hate going to her parents'. Her father is set on the same clock as me, only 10 or 15 minutes ahead. Also, he reads in the toilet. When I sit down, the seat is always warm and a little sticky. The image of her father pooing that this brings up is just horrible."

Ian, 29, in a relationship, Aberdeen

DINNER WITH HER FRIENDS

You are both having dinner at her friends' place. The evening is going well...
that is, until a desperate urge to poo comes over you.

DIFFICULTY

SOLUTION: THE ESTATE AGENT

1. Flatter her friends' taste and tell them that their — perfectly ordinary — apartment reminds you of the "Home by Van Hayuut" style (famous Dutch architect that you made up). Don't worry, nobody will suspect you out because everybody loves flattery.
2. Marvel at their intercom: "Such an interesting design! It's fabulous!" Go on in the same vein about their light switches.
3. Then suddenly exclaim: "Oh my God! I bet your toilet is a John Batt! I absolutely must have a look."
4. Once you are gone, her friends will talk about you behind your back.
5. Do your deed quickly (SPEED rule).
6. Come back to the table and report that the toilet isn't a John Batt, but rather Kray Woods, which is even more fabulous. They will just love you. Mission doubly accomplished.

EXPERT'S OPINION

"Don't get carried away by your fake role — unless you actually are an interior design expert or your girlfriend has especially stupid friends."

TESTIMONIAL

"Her friends are really stingy: they buy only single-sheet toilet paper. It tears even when you handle it carefully. I hate it. Now, when they visit, I remove all toilet paper from our two toilets so that they have to struggle like I do. They don't dare ask for paper. It always makes me laugh on the inside when they gingerly walk back into the room, refusing to sit down."

Damian, 24, in a relationship, Sheffield

You take the tube to go to a restaurant you booked for dinner. You are still far from your destination, but you can't wait... you need to go to the loo immediately.

DIFFICULTY

SOLUTION: THE FOLDING SEAT

1. Stay stone-faced (COMPOSURE rule), and don't lose precious time looking for a toilet in the carriage; it's the underground, not a train.
2. Step to another part of the carriage under the pretext that you want to check the map to make sure you're going in the right direction.
3. Sit on the folding seat and do your deed.
4. Return to her and exit the train under the pretext that you took the wrong line. Do it quickly: according to scientific studies, the odour spreads at a constant speed of 32.6 km/h on a moving train. Considering the size of the carriage, you don't have much time.

EXPERT'S OPINION

"One of my clients did this in Paris. He was in a carriage that was nearly empty, but he didn't know that the train was 100m away from one of the busiest stations of the Paris Metro. When the door opened, he was faced with over 30 passengers while he was doing his deed. At the next station, the carriage emptied. He was caught on CCTV and taken in for questioning. The only thing that saved him was France's ancient 'right to poo' law."

TESTIMONIAL

"I needed to go so badly I was going crazy. I was like a chicken locked inside a spinning washing machine. When I saw the emergency stop handle, I saw a toilet flush and instinctively pulled it. Result: 18 hours of police detention. My little victory: after I went to the toilet at the police station, the cops couldn't go in there for at least two hours."

Matthew, 24, single, London

COMING BACK FROM A WEEKEND GETAWAY

You spent a wonderful weekend together: candlelit dinners, the best nightclubs, expensive hotels... You kept up appearances by not going to the toilet all weekend, but on the road back you reach saturation point. She is driving, and you are silently suffering next to her.

DIFFICULTY

SOLUTION: DRIVING LESSONS

1. Don't delay a trip to the toilet any longer; you have already put your health and intestines in danger with your perilous abstinence.
2. When you see a sign for an upcoming service station, say to her: "This is already the fourth time that you didn't use the signal when overtaking!"
3. Go on: "Careful, you are over speed limit by 1 mph!"
4. Add: "Could you drive a bit more to the right?"
5. At this point she's surely had it (or she's deaf). She will exit at the next service station and yell: "You drive then!"
6. Tell her you want to get her something to apologize, like ice cream or coffee.
7. Go inside and go to the toilet discreetly (INVISIBILITY rule). Do your deed quickly (SPEED rule).
8. Go back to the car.

EXPERT'S OPINION

"One of my patients used this method but his girlfriend didn't stop at the service station. He had to make a badly disguised 'pit stop' at an SOS bollard."

TESTIMONIAL

"I forgot to bring the ice cream I had promised her. She left me at the service station. I would like to use this book to ask Cindy to kindly return my car; I need it to go to work."

Benjamin, 26, single, Exeter

YOU ARE WALKING HER DOG

She's asked you to walk her dog while she gets ready (when you think about it, it was probably her technique to get rid of you so she could go to the toilet!) You leave the flat, with the dog on his lead. The dog soon relieves himself. Seeing him unleashes the same urge in you.

DIFFICULTY

SOLUTION: THE STICK

1. Go to the nearest bar or restaurant.
2. Go to the toilet discreetly, and bring the dog with you (INTIMACY and INVISIBILITY rule combo).
3. Go to the stall and sit down.
4. Make the dog sit between your legs, with his head towards the door.
5. Take the toilet brush.
6. Put the handle of the toilet brush into the dog's mouth to prevent him from barking. Move it around so that he takes it as a game. Say to the dog as quietly as possible: "Good dog, you like your stick, don't you! Good boy!" If the dog gets too excited, bind him up with toilet paper.
7. Do your deed rapidly (SPEED rule).
8. Leave the toilet as if nothing's happened. (SECRECY rule)

EXPERT'S OPINION

"Even if you can't hold it in anymore and you find yourself next to a sand pit intended for dog excrement, don't even think about it!"

TESTIMONIAL

"I agreed to walk Max, Julie's dog. When I had to go to the toilet, it turned into a complete mess. While I was at it, the dog was barking, licked the walls and even pissed on my feet. When we came back, she gave him a big kiss, even though his tongue was sticking out. Ever since then I always brush my teeth nine times after we kiss."

Evan, 34, in a relationship, Cardiff

YOU HAVE TO OPEN THE DOOR FOR HER LIKE A GENTLEMAN

You spent an evening together and you were a perfect gentleman the whole time. You are driving back, and she now expects you to come around the car to open the door for her when you arrive. You, however, just want to bolt to the toilet as soon as you can.

DIFFICULTY

SOLUTION: ALI BABA'S CAVE

1. Step out of the car without any sign of distress (COMPOSURE rule).
2. Go around the back of the car so she doesn't see that you are folded in pain.
3. Open the boot of the car and sit on the edge of it with your bum hanging out (SPEED rule).
4. Do your deed ultra fast (otherwise she will wonder what's going on and get out of the car).
5. Find a road map, a safety jacket... anything you can use to wipe yourself with.
6. Go towards her door, look at her with a big smile and open the door for her as if she were a princess.
7. Guide her to the front end of the car (SECURITY rule).

   Careful: never use this method with cars that have a tailgate. You would be visible while doing your deed, which defeats the purpose.

EXPERT'S OPINION

"I was once in a Ferrari on a date. Its owner was taken with an urgent need to poo. This dummy applied the method perfectly, except that the engine is in the back and the boot is in front. I could see everything... What an idiot."

TESTIMONIAL

"I sat in the boot. As I love picnics, I always have picnic equipment in the car. I did my deed in an empty ice box that I closed behind me, and I wiped up with 'plum blossom' paper cocktail napkins."

Tony, 36, married, Barnstaple

YOU ARE ILL

You have gastroenteritis, most definitely the worst possible situation you can encounter. You put your powers of seduction in jeopardy every ten minutes, as you need to run to the toilet. You must urgently find a way to be away from her for a few hours so that you can relieve yourself.

DIFFICULTY

SOLUTION: THE PAYOFF

1. When you get out of the toilet, take advantage of the short time before you'll have to return to run as fast as you can to the nearest cash point machine.
2. Withdraw £1,000.
3. Give her the £1,000 and tell her to go shopping. Our tests suggest that her face will light up with pure joy.
4. She will spend £200 per hour on average, which gives you five hours to get some relief. If five hours isn't enough, don't hesitate for a second. Go and withdraw a further £1,000 and repeat the operation.
5. A note to our female readers: This solution may seem a bit sexist so we apologise for that (you will notice that other solutions suggested in this book were not at all sexist). However, this is not the case; it is merely the only efficient technique that we have found in our extensive research to ensure a prolonged absence.

EXPERT'S OPINION

"One of my patients applied this technique, but he was uncovered. She was very understanding and worried, so with the £500 that he gave her, she bought him two pallets of toilet paper."

TESTIMONIAL

"It was a bad one. I had to go every ten minutes. It smelled so bad that three neighbours convened in the corridor. They called a plumber. They were convinced that the central plumbing had exploded. They were looking for a leak. They followed the smell and found me. I had to pay the plumber."

Frank, 34, single, Sandwich

BONUS: HOW TO BUY 10 MINUTES

After three years of dilligently applying our own techniques we realized that sometimes a bit more time was needed to find an ideal window of opportunity to execute them. We approached Dr Chouy and a fitness specialist.

Our goal: To create a method that would help 'gain' ten minutes before one absolutely must go to the toilet.

Result: We came up with an exclusive method – "Zen Body and Spirit" – that helps control internal organs and delays by exactly ten minutes the urge to go to the toilet. However, you should note that this method is a time bomb: on precisely the eleventh minute, the urge comes back with triple force. Few men have been able to resist it (according to our tests).

Step 1: Control Your Spirit

Stand with your legs apart and place your hands on your lower abdomen. Imagine that your abdomen is expanding and that there is still a lot of room there.

Step 2: Channel Your Energy

Inhale and raise your arms upwards. Spread your legs. Stay in this position and imagine that you are the most powerful dam in the world and nothing can break you. Tell yourself that you are so solid that not even torrential rain, tree trunks or a terrible mud flood could crack you.

Step 3: Re-center

Lie on your back, fold your legs and bring them to your chest. Hug your knees with your hands to bring them as closely as possible to your chest. You are now one unit and your whole body is under your control.

BONUS: YOUR RELATIONSHIP AND THE TOILET

A test to check the sanitary-sentimental health of your relationship.

Is your relationship in danger? You will get a clear and reliable answer by answering the following questions.

QUESTION 1

Have you ever looked her in the eyes after a meal and told her: "I have to go so badly it's almost out!"

☐ YES ☐ NO

QUESTION 2

When you are in the supermarket together, it's not unusual to hear you discuss the advantages and disadvantages of different toilet paper brands: "I prefer this one, it's much softer", "No, not that one, it's rough", "Oh no, not that thin one, it tears every time," "I love the perfumed one, it's so refreshing".

☐ YES ☐ NO

QUESTION 3

Have you ever come back from the shop bragging about having purchased 224 rolls of paper for the price of 166 because they had a 'Big Boy Promotion'?

☐ YES ☐ NO

QUESTION 4

The toilet is in the bathroom, and it happens regularly that while one is brushing their teeth, the other is doing their deed.

☐ YES ☐ NO

QUESTION 5

Have you ever phoned your partner from the toilet while you were relieving yourself, so that she heard you do it?

☐ YES ☐ NO

QUESTION 6

There is no more toilet paper. Do you yell: "Can someone bring me some toilet paper?"

☐ YES ☐ NO

QUESTION 7

Have you ever had bean salad followed by cabbage before a romantic evening?

☐ YES ☐ NO

QUESTION 8

You have just done your deed and it smells very bad. You run all over the flat and spray it with an entire bottle of Coconut Breeze air freshener.

☐ YES ☐ NO

QUESTION 9

You let a fart pop out. You laugh and wave your arms to disperse the smell, but you are pretty proud of yourself.

☐ YES ☐ NO

QUESTION 10

You think it's pretty funny to leave the bathroom with toilet paper wrapped over your eyes, yelling that you are Zorro and waving the toilet brush in the air like a sword?

☐ YES ☐ NO

1) Yes: 3 toilet paper rolls   No: 0 toilet paper rolls
2) Yes: 1 toilet paper rolls   No: 0 toilet paper rolls
3) Yes: 1 toilet paper rolls   No: 0 toilet paper rolls
4) Yes: 6 toilet paper rolls   No: 0 toilet paper rolls
5) Yes: 3 toilet paper rolls   No: 0 toilet paper rolls
6) Yes: 2 toilet paper rolls   No: 0 toilet paper rolls
7) Yes: 1 toilet paper rolls   No: 0 toilet paper rolls
8) Yes: 4 toilet paper rolls   No: 0 toilet paper rolls
9) Yes: 3 toilet paper rolls   No: 0 toilet paper rolls
10) Yes: 6 toilet paper rolls   No: 0 toilet paper rolls

Count your toilet paper rolls and analyse your results:

0 toilet paper rolls – Bravo, you are an expert! You don't mix love and toilets; you have a bright future together.

From 1 to 29 toilet paper rolls – Your relationship is in danger. You should take a deep, hard look at it. You shouldn't be surprised if you find yourself single in a few days, chased out of your love nest with a toilet brush, toilet paper rolls flying.

30 toilet paper rolls – We only have one question for you: how did you two even end up in a relationship?

QUALITY GUARANTEE

These methods were tested under the ISO-WC 3003 standard.

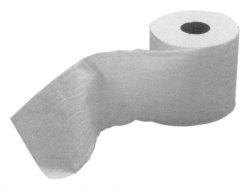

Each technique was tested three times.

Certification Authority: QPWC31.12 Dep8, Los Angeles (USA)
In this illustration, the certification authority auditor, John Krayd,
is testing a technique from the chapter "At her place".

CONCLUSION

You finished this book. You learned that it is possible to act on your toilet problems and thus change your life. However, we would like to emphasize the importance of introspection and working towards accepting that all your previous romantic issues should probably be attributed to your bad toilet behaviour. You cannot go on in life if you do not accept your past. We hope that your perspective on romantic relationships has changed by reading this book. You should be able to trust us by now: believe us, believe in yourself and you will succeed!

In the abundance of information that we have transmitted to you, there is one thing you should remember above all, and that is that there can be no long term relationship nor successful dates without proper management of toilet use. This may have surprised you at first – that is normal – but we have no doubt that you are now convinced. Together we have reviewed all the situations that could end your relationship. Now it is time for action. Good luck!

ONE LAST PIECE OF ADVICE

Even when you are not in a relationship, you should keep doing your exercises daily. Practice repeatedly, run through simulations of the situations described in this book with your close friends or family... In short: train constantly so that you will be ready when it counts, because after that there will be no margin of error.

If you are in a relationship, we have no doubt that our advice will do the trick and that you will stay with your partner for the long haul. However, don't forget to take advantage of any absences to practice our techniques. Be careful and don't get caught in your living room with three rolls of toilet paper, a toilet brush and a shirt that smells of air freshener.